Sputnikolor Dreams

Ian Lynn Moore, I

Copyright © 2012 Ian Lynn Moore, I

All rights reserved.

ISBN-13: 978-1480027152
(CreateSpace-Assigned)

ISBN-10: 1480027154

Cover Art by Jorge Salazar (DMS 2010)

DEDICATION

To all my students at
Paul Laurence Dunbar Middle School for Innovation
Past, Present, & Future

Go Mad Dog Nation

CONTENTS

Acknowledgments   iv
1   The Law and the Giants   6 - 37

Sputnikolor Dreams	6
Motion	8
Molecules	10
Quantum Reality	11
Energy Flows	12
Giants	13
P	14
I Am	15
Running	16
Life	17
Sputnik	18
Set Me Free	20
Hope	22
Under the Sod	26
666	27
Forget	28
Power	29
Help Me	30
Loud	31
Where the Corpses Lay	32
Relativity	35
The Song of Science	36

2 The Songs of Science   38 - 91

Lab Room Blitz   40
Scientific Delight   44
Conversation   47
N- a – C – l   49
Precipitation   52
Scientific   54
Feel Like Reactin'   55
This Electricity   57
Atomic House   62
Photon Baby   64
Metalloid   65
Wave   67
Mr. Moore   69
Gravity's Not a Friend   71
Transverse Waves   73
Sail Your Boat   76
Welcome to the Lab Room   78
Cellular   79
Red Hot   82
You Matter   84
Elements   87
Gravity   89

3 The Truth According to Mr. S'More   92 - 130

SOL	94
Fourteen	96
Rapturous Morning	98
The Truth About Water	99
Deer	101
Punnett Squares	102
Meal Ticket	103
Green Hawaiian	104
Rusty Wire	107
The Epistle to Kay, Who's No Longer Here	108
If Only	110
Voiceless	111
The Epistle to Ray, in Prison	112
The Congregation of the Mighty	115
Hornets	117
Cosmos Cake	118
Friendly Fire	119
Option 7 and the CBA's	120
Wire	123
Birthday Cake	124
Cellular Secrets	128
Fire with Fire	129

About the Author   132

ACKNOWLEDGMENTS

This effort sprang out of my desire to find fresh and intriguing ways for my students to internalize the scientific concepts I present in class. Without my students there would be no Sputnikolor Dreams. Thank you Dunbar!

Above my students I need have to thank my mom, Elinor H. M. Davis, who never stopped believing in me in spite of the evidence.

Second, but not by much, my wife Deborah Goulette Moore, who has loved and supported me for twenty years and bugged me for just as long to write.

Thank you Dee Brown, the author of The Trials and Tribulations of a Fried Bologna Sandwich and several other books and screen plays, who mentored me through the process of producing Sputnikolor Dreams.

Thanks to Susan McLawhorne, who eagerly agreed to edit for me. She encouraged me and kept me on task even when some of what I gave her was unreadable dribble.

Cover Art: Jorge Salazar

THE LAW AND THE GIANTS

Sputnikolor Dreams

Sputnikolor Dreams

Thrust across October nights
A whiskered orb the world ignites
Imagination's shackles loosed
The race to the abyss ensues

Atmospheric limits reached
Then like hurricane soaked levies breached
And pierced a gateway to the stars
Breaking from cerebral bars

Through the ether luminous
Suspending the cosmic abyss
Casting brilliant novel hues
Changing how we live, and learn, and do

No longer tethered by atmospheres
Nor chained by superstitious fears
With stones hewn out by Giant's hands
On foundations laid by the Son of Man

They trickle in one by one
And take their place beneath the sun
Among the ghosts the haunt these halls
And answer wisdom's soulful call

Most of their names I've long forgotten

Though some have soared and some have fallen

But all I've sent out to the world

I hope for dreams in Sputnikolor.

Motion

Matter in motion, particles flowing
The hotter they get, the faster they're going

Atoms in solids feel the vibration
As they warm they swarm 'cross the nation
There's fluid motion, gas, and liquids
Charged ions collide in plasmas

My science matters, got what you're after
Open your mind and look for what happens
My science matters, ain't nothin' better
Explore the cosmos, knowledge you'll capture

Four basic forces keep planets in courses
Atoms connected, magnetic electric
Matter is energy, we always conserve it
And just momentum there's no destroyer

Positive protons and neutral neutrons
Are circled around negative 'lectrons

Molecules

Molecules
Exchanging electrons
Building the stuff of creation
Electromagnetic affinity
Inside you and me
Outlasting eternity.

Quantum Reality

Matter energy

Energy matter

The flux of everything that we know

In a perpetual state of inexistence

Quantum reality

Matter energy

Energy matter

Energy Flows

She said "Some days I got potential,
Thermal, atomic and gravitational
I look again and I'm all kinetic,
Elastic, chemical, electromagnetic
Always flippin' back and forth,
On a never endin' course.
Kinetic to potential and then back again
Movin' like a pendulum, back and for th it'll neva end.
It's not like I'm always movin' and grovin'
Sometimes I'm just chillin', you know, time killin'
Storin' up that energy, just to let it go
Detroit leanin', cruisin' down the road
If there's a vibration, that's energy flowin'
But when you're sittin' still you're all the while knowin'
That pretty soon you gotta look up and get up,
And post up or shut up
 Cause you know

All energy flows
You know it goes forever
It goes on and on
On and on it goes
Potential and kinetic
All energy flows

Giants

Copernicus sees

Kepler calculates

Galileo thrust the doors open wide

Newton stands as judge and jury

Maxwell

Einstein

Hawking

P

P is momentum

Velocity times the mass

It's always conserved

I Am

I am Energy
Everlasting, immortal me
I spoke and there is
I breathed life into Apollo and Ra
From the dust of the universe I gathered them
And cast them on the canvas of space/time
With my pierced hands
I am clothed in dangerous hues
Of electromagnetic splendor
That burst organic lattice
Into a rouge super nova
I am Energy.

Running

Energy is food
It is either stored in cans
Or keeps me running

Life

Assuming life's but chemicals
Breath is an exchange of gases
A periodic function
Of a few elements
Combine… Recombine
Then is there love?
Is it real?
Who knows?
Me?

                                                                      Me!
                                                                 I know.
                                                             I'll tell you
                                                         Or ask a child.
                                           No truth matters more.
                                         Love is the breath of God.
                                     His gift to us, ours to share,
                        After He scooped us from the clay;
                             Divine Electromagnetism

Sputnik

Sputnik
Bing… bing
A new era
Racing for the moon
Sputnik

Set Me Free

Hey there Mr. Newton,
Why won't you please just set me free,
I've got two tickets to the moon
But there's this thing called gravity
That keeps my face down on the ground
And I can barely see the world crashing down

Hey there Mr. Newton
You can keep your damn apple tree
I've traveled all around the world
But there's somewhere I'd rather be
Your gravity ain't never been a friend
It just makes the world come crashing down

Hey there Mr. Newton,
You let your giants down
You need to calibrate your abacus
There must be a mistake
But as you calculate trajectory
I'm stuck here as the world comes crashing down

Hey there Mr. Newton
Is there a court to hear my plea
Because your laws were made for breaking

And I'll gladly pay the fee

Or am I just a hired jester

Dancing while the world around crashes down

Hey there Mr. Newton

You see there's something else I found

That keeps this big blue ball a spinnnin'

And the planets whirlin' round

You can't calculate it's where-a-bouts

By some trajectory

Hey there Mr. Newton

Is there not an answer key

I got no use for gravity

It ain't never been friend to me.

It keeps me too close to reality.

Safe here on the ground where I can't see.

Hope

Teaching really is a masochistic profession. It seems like there is always someone or something against you. The administration is breathing down your neck about some kind of paperwork, parents are either on you because your class is too hard or too easy or you are being unfair to their kid. The kids, especially the kids, fight you every step of the way from the second they walk in the door. But, we keep signing the contracts, we keep showing up to work, we keep reading this book or that, and going those conference trying to stay on top of our game so that we can impact the life of that proverbial "one kid." I know its hard to believe, but teachers really aren't in it for the money and public prestige. Maybe, for the summers, snow days and Christmas break, but really because we hold fast a hope for tomorrow.

Most of us love what we do but, there is always someone in class who NEVER has a pencil, their notebook, their homework, their book, or, I'm pretty sure, their brain. Sometimes these kids are goofy and lovable, in spite of their in ability to breathe without someone reminding them every few minutes. Others are combative, like they are doing me a favor by just showing to class and their gift should be reciprocated by the me letting them do whatever disruptive behavior they choose at any moment, all while maintaining an A/B average. These militants are pretty rare but they make their mark on history and when the opportunity to turn the tables without risking a jaunt in the state penitentiary one tends to pounce like a kitten on a bug.

A Van de Graff generator, is the middle school version of "Ride the Lightning." "Can I get a volunteer?" Of coarse, the girl with long hair gets a chance to look like character from the "Mod Squad." If everything is working right every hair on her head will stick straight up like rays from the sun. Any embarrassment they might feel is always outweighed by their glee at seeing what is actually happening. This rather benign demonstration sets the stage for the main event. Now, even my militant student wants to hone in on this action, besides electricity and sparks are cool no matter who is in the audience. .

"Larry, come on down!" "step up on the stool, put your hand on the top of the generator and don't take it off until I tell you." "You don't have a heart condition of any kind do you? Good." "Any problems with randomly wetting yourself?" " You might after this."

At this point the fear begins to build and overtake his completion. Flashes of his eight school years of mischief begin a light speed slide show in his mind and he at least regrets raising his hand and blurting out "Me, pick Me!" His anxiety compounded by the sadistic gleam in my eyes as I reach for the switch.

I can't resist asking, "Did you ever see <u>The Green Mile?</u>" followed by an "ezzzit" electrical sound and mini seizure, temping poor Larry's incontinence.

"Is Larry a positive person or negative?" I ask the class.

"Negative!" is the landslide response. Honestly it wouldn't matter if Mother Theresa was connected to the generator they always answer negative, so there are no real self esteem issues at stake here.

"We'll not anymore. He is the most positive person in the room."

"What is Larry made of?"

"Muscles and bones?"

"What are they made of?"

"Cells?"

"Yes, but smaller."

"Atoms!"

"Right, but what are atoms made of"

"Protons, neutrons and electrons."

"OK, what's the difference between them?"

If I'm lucky the class will answer something to the effect of, "protons are positive, neutrons are neutral and they are in the nucleus, electrons are negative and surround the nucleus."

All the while, Larry is standing there connected to the generator and, by now, loose clothing is beginning to levitate.

"What are the charges of the particles that make him up?"

"Positive, neutral and negative"

"So, what would have to happen for him to be more positive?"

"He'd have to gain protons"

"That would change the actual elements that he is made of. Did we do that?

"No"

"If we can't add protons, what can we take away to make him more positive?"

"Electrons!"

"Electrons, right. The Van de Graff generator strips away electrons leaving an unbalanced ratio of positive to negative charges making Larry more positive."

Larry's fillings are tingling and there is an audible crackle in the air around him.

"How can we know that he has an unbalanced electrical charge? What do you already know about magnetism and like and opposite poles?"

"So, 'like' charged objects will repel each other. Kind of like every strand of hair, his hoodie strings and even the lint on his sleeve? Well that is half the story, like charges repel but what about unlike charges?" By this time I am standing right next to Larry and I edge my elbow out towards his arm and "pow." A spark jumps like something from a champion spark plug commercial. Larry jumps and pulls his hand of the generator and get another bite. The room erupts and I've satisfy my thrust.

In reality, I know the spark hurts me much more than it hurts Larry, having been on both sides of this demonstration. But those several minutes while I have him in my clutches are priceless and more often than not, the spark I deliver that day silences the militant and awakens that one kid I am able to reach, making all the pain worth it.

Under the Sod

Souls languish in suburban squalor
Manicured lawns and SUVs
Upon the treadmill we climb
Into the stagnant expense of force

Round and round and round
But our spinning wheels never touch the ground
Through virtual landscapes where nature can't spoil
And sweat offers no solace between the bits and bites

Choking on breath of leaf blowers and grills
Autumn scarcely finds the earth
Plucked and tucked 'til nothing's left
Of what creation formed at birth

Where is what use to be
Beneath the thin stretched sod
When we've spent our lives,
From womb to grave,
Erasing the finger print of God

666

Six, six, six: carbon

Six hundred and sixty-six

The number of man

Forget

Still, I can't forget your name.
When everyone else is all but faded
Space has clouded, time has jaded.
What makes your not the same?

I wonder if it's me you blame
Or have I chosen to be haunted
Still, I can't forget your name.
When everyone else is all but faded

Yours was such a dirty fame
The taste of blue steel, then lead.
You must have had it in your head
Your tormentor you would tame.

Still, I can't forget your name.

Power

Power
Raw energy
Before creation "I am"
Everlasting and Immortal
The very breath of God

Help Me

I walked in the lab on a Monday mornin'
Didn't know what to expect so it came without warnin'
Boilin', bubblin' in a chemical brew
Come on teacher man won't you show me what to do?

Tuesday came, thought it would be the same
So it blew me away when the sound waves came
They rattled and rolled and they shook the floor
The learnin' flowed and rolled out the door

On Wednesday I thought I could sit and relax
But I found myself on Isaac Newton's tracks
Gravity was there and tried to hold me down
Be the laws of motion kept me spinnin' round

I got off the bus and I looked at my phone
It was only Thursday and I started to moan
I shuffled on into my science class
Instead of a bell there was a hydrogen blast

TGIF and the tardy bell rang
It dawned on me that I had learned while I sang
This class is fun and in spite what I heard
Science I found is an action word.

Loud

Explosions are cool
Potential energy gone
Kinetic and loud

Where the Corpses Lay

Out here,
Along an row of ancient locust poles
Thrust into the earth long before this generation
Where the blackberries and green-briars draw their DMZ
With their barbed, iron cousin
Who's rust brown talons conspire
With emergency rooms and pharmaceutical companies
Against boys and grown men
Who dare to forage for adrenaline
Out here.

Just inside the gate
Where we often pass
Under which my dog launches his jihad
Against all that is feral and unbridled,
Masterless beasts who answer to God, alone.
Out on the edge of the manicured
The ebb of the civilized,
At the twilight of the tame,
Out here,
Just inside the gate.

Under a pile of scrap
The refuse of our global dependency

Old growth shipping pallets
Sun bleached and splintered
They've traversed the globe
Only to melt back into eternity
Here in my back yard
Golden-rod reaches through the slats
These are the raw materials of a barracks
to quarter our holy warrior
Between his skirmishes,
Out here,
Just inside the gate,
Under the scrap pile.

In the dust
With the wisps of dead fescue
Where the pallets once lay
Lay the still twitching
No longer copperheads
Glistening in the morning sun
The grass still wet with dew
Their only crime was just to be
To encroach a foot or two beyond.
Shoulder slung, blue steel and walnut
Warm from projectile friction
And red-orange flash
Broken at the breech and empty

Powder still burning in my nostrils
I'd sent for my gun from second nature
Unbridled, un-mastered, even by God.
Out here,
Just inside the gate,
Under the scrap pile,
In the dust.

Where the corpses lay
Shot showered from confident contentment
Yet still conflicted
And plagued by pangs of disappointment
And I'd do it again without thought, without remorse,
With fierce resolve and fearsome savagery
But still tinged with sorrow
That there is no peace between wild and not
That there's been no Evolution,
I am who was created
We are children of Eden and our destiny sealed
His to bruise my heal and I his head

Out here,
Just inside the gate,
Under the scrap pile,
In the dust,
Where the corpses lay.

Relativity

E is m c square

Relativity in chalk

The fabric of time

The Song of Science

Setting fire to minds
For twenty-two days she sang
The Song of Science

Sputnikolor Dreams

Ian Lynn Moore, I

SONGS OF SCIENCE

Sputnikolor Dreams

Scientific Delight

I said a hip hop hip a hippadiddi
Hip hip hoppin' ya don't stop a rocking
From the bang of creation
There's been a relation
Between physics and chemistry.

Now what you'll hear is on the test
I'm really not insane
And me, the mike and all my friends
Are gonna try to rock your brain
Ya see I am Mr. Moore and I'd like to say "Hi Y'all"
To the black, to the white, the brown, and the yella,
And all the people out in the hall.

I say, "Title, purpose, hypothesis"
Got a little rhythm and it goes like this
In the hood with a materials list,
All my peeps in scientific bliss.
(The) procedure next, one two three.
Pick your data and follow me
Charts and graphs havin' too much fun,
Turn it all around for you conclusion.

And it on and a on And on, on and on and

And the method don't stop 'til the break of dawn

I said M-E-T-H-O-D,

It's the scientific method gonna help you see

You know it's going down in history

As the fly-est way to question that will ever be

I'm feeling the highs, you're feeling the lows

The scientific method gets into your toes.

You got protons, neutrons,

Electrons moving in…

Atomic structure

Is where we'll begin

There's atomic numbers and atomic mass,

Solids, liquids, plasma, gas

Periodic table with periodic groups,

Organizing matter like a rummy suit

You got lanthanides and actinides

Alkali metals and noble gas,

Alkaline earth and halogens

Listen up dogs cause I talking real fast

Chemical Bonds with electrons

Orbitin' atoms with neutral neutrons

There's HCl and CO_2

A nuclear force that sticks like glue

I got more science than I could ever do.

Rock the laboratory like 2 Live Crew

Makin' more money than I'll ever spend

Rappin' about the Science with all my friends

Have you ever been ova a friend's house to eat

And the food just ain't no good

You got rotten tomatoes and burned potatoes

And the chicken tastes like wood

Well it's all because of some simple reactions

That have been misunderstood

So spend some time in the kitchen

And start payin' attention

To the science of the hood

You see heat causes evaporation

And it makes some things combust.

So, if you leave it on the stove too long

You might as well eat rust.

You see O_2 causes food to rot

So, you might want to inhibitate,

But if you don't you might find out

You waited all too late

'Cause if you see b-u-b --- b-l-e

It's a sign its reacting, that's chemistry

Hot or cold that's energy

A change in color is what you see

If it smells or if it burns

Chemical bonds is what you've learned

A catalyst can change the speed,

But filling valance levels is all you need

From the Sugar Hill Gang's "Rapper's Delight"

The Lab Room Blitz

Well, It's been getting so hard
Keeping up with homework you give to me,
The work is getting so strange
I'd like you to (ex)splain some stuff to me

    OH, I see a kid at the back
    As a matter of fact his eyes are bright as the sun
    And the girl in the corner let no one ignore her
    'Cause she knows that labs are fun

Oh Yeh, it was like lightning,
Everybody was writin'
And the Bunsen was burnin',
And they all started learnin'
Yeah, Yeah, Yeah, Yeah, Yeah
And the rat at the back said
Everyone attack
And it turned into a lab room blitz
And the teacher in the corner said
Boy, I wanna warn ya,
It'll turn into a lab room blitz
Lab room blitz

Matter and energy can be neither created nor destroyed in an action or reaction

I'm reaching out for knowledge
And knowledge is what science does for me

some times I use a catalyst,
other times an inhibitor is what I need.

    And the kid in the back
    Has got a book to crack
    As he raises his hands to the sky
    And the girl in the corner
    Says everyone's a learner
    All you got to do is open your eyes

Oh yeah, it was electric,
So chemically hectic
And the liquid starts boilin',
And gasses were formin'
Yeah, Yeah, Yeah, Yeah, Yeah
And the hamster at the back said,
"Everyone attack,"
and it turned into a lab room blitz
And the teacher in the corner said
"Boy, I wanna warn ya,
It's gonna turn into a lab room blitz."
Lab room blitz

Energy is he ability to do work
Work is the movement of mass over a distance
Mass is the measurement of the amount of matter in a substance
Matter is made of tiny particles that are in constant motion.
The average kinetic energy of those particles is determined by temperature.

Oh Yeah, it was like lightning,
And so enlightenin'
And there was nobody sleepin'
And they're brains started wrinklin'
Yeah, Yeah, Yeah, Yeah, Yeah

    And the rat at the back said
    "Everyone attack"
    And it turned into a lab room blitz
    And the teacher in the corner said
    "Boy, I wanna warn ya,
    It'll turn into a lab room blitz."
    lab room blitz

This, it's the lab room blitz,
This, it's the lab room blitz
This, it's the lab room blitz,

The particles of a solid only vibrate in place
In liquid the particle have enough energy to around each other but not away and take the shape of their container
The energy in gas particles allow them to flow freely and completely defuse throughout their container.
Melting and boiling points are periodic properties of matter

From Sweet's "Ballroom Blitz"

Conversation

I wanna have a little conversation about action, please
You'll have a little less aggravation if you listen to me!

For every up there's an equal down
That's the law that Mr. Newton found
So, come on kids and take a rocket ride with me
A rocket ride with me.

Open up your eyes and listen to the music
Drifting off like a fade away
For every action there's an equal and opposite reaction

I wanna have a little conversation about action, please
You'll have a little less aggravation once you finally see

For every up there's an equal down
It's a law of motion Newton found
So, come on kids and take a rocket ride with me
A rocket ride with me.

Come on y'all I ain't tired of talking
So, grab your coat and I can teach while you're walkin'
Come on, come on
Come on, come on

Listen up while I try to articulate

When you push on the ground it pushes back on you

I wanna have a little conversation about action, please

You'll have a little less aggravation when your mind's set free.

For every up there's an equal down

It's a law of motion Newton found

So, come on kids and take a rocket ride with me

A rocket ride with me.

From Elvis Presley's "Conversation"

N-a-C-l

Hydrogen

That's just floating around

Bonds with chlorine

To make HCl

And there's Sodium

Hooked to a H and an O

It makes sodium

Hydroxide.

When those two

Ionic compounds meet

There's a reaction

And some atoms switch place

H positive

Hooks with OH negative

You've got H_2O

and also…

You know I'm talkin' 'bout NaCl

Its fun to play with some, NaCl

It's got everything

For your chemistry needs

It's even good on collard greens!

You know I'm talkin' 'bout, NaCl

You know you gotta have it, NaCl

It melts the ice of the road.

It dissolves a slug.

Throw it over your shoulder for luck!

Salt is

An ionic compound

Na's positive

It gave it's 'lectrons away

Cl gave them

A new place to stay

So, that a zero

Net oxidation.

Electrons

Make the whole thing go down

Their charge is negative

And they're flowin' around

If you lose one

It's a positive oxidation

If you gain one

Now you're now more negative.

The formation

Of salt is a great example

Of a reaction

Where two elements switch bonds

NaOH

Plus HCl

Become NaCl

And water.

Anytime

Two elements switch in a bond

And you get water

A precipitate or salt

The reaction

Has a specific name

It's a double displacement reaction.

You know I'm talkin' 'bout, NaCl.

You know you gotta have it, NaCl.

N-a-C-l

From The Village People's "YMCA"

Precipitation

Oh, yeah!
Its precipitation!

Celebrate good times, come on! (its precipitation)
Celebrate good times, come on! (its precipitation)

You know its rainin' all around the world
Precipitation that happens all the year
Forming oceans, lakes and rivers too
The water cycle bringin' water to you

Come on now

Precipitation
You know there would be no life if we didn't have rain
Precipitation
Lets all go out side and play in the rain

It's time to talk about weather
Effecting you, its H_2O treasure

Its rainin' all around the world
Come on!

Oh, yeah,

Its precipitation

Oh, yeah

Pre-cip-i-ta-tion, come on!

It's a precipitation

Pre-cip-i-ta-tion, come on!

Let's precipitate

You know it might rain all night

Precipitate, it's all right

You know it might rain all night

Precipitate, it's all right

Its rainin'...

From Cool and the Gang's "Celebration"

Scientific

Very scientific, writing' in my log
Very scientific, knowledge for us all
Identify the problem; tell what you what to know.
Then give your hypothesis, its always your best guess.

When you try to figure out
Things you don't understand
With an organized plan
It's the Scientific method way

Very scientific, protect your face and hands
Try to solve the problem, list all the things you'll need.
Keepin' all the data so it's all easy to read
You don't wanna save me, sad is my song

Very scientific, got one thing more to say
Very scientific, the answers on its way
Conclusion form from the knowledge that you gain
Repeat the steps 2-3-4, then you do it all again

From Stevie Wonder's "Superstitious"

Feel Like Reactin'

You know there's five reactions
Synthesis and combustibility
Decomposition and displacement
Double and single you see

But mass remains the same
Conservation names the game

You make me feel like reactin'
I'm gonna React the night away
You make me feel like reactin'
I'm gonna React the night away
You make feel like reactin'
I feel like reactin' reactin' react the night away
I feel like reactin' reactin' ahhh

Synthesis comes together
Decomposition breaks down
An element's replaced and it's a single displace
If there's two, a double is what its gotta be

Combustion is the way to go
If you wanna see it glow

You make me feel like reactin'
I'm gonna react the night away
You make me feel like reactin'
I'm gonna react the night away
You make feel like reactin'
I feel like reactin' reactin' React the night away
I feel like reactin' reactin' ahhh

Catalysts can speed up things
Inhibitors slow it down
Exothermic lets go of energy
Endothermic absorbs
Its all about electron flow
Oxidation tells which way they goes

You make me feel like reactin' I wanna react the night away
You make me feel like reactin' I'm gonna React my life away
I feel like reactin' reactin' react the night away
I feel like reactin' reactin' react the night away
I feel like reactin' reactin' ahhh

And electrons flow they know which way to go
You make me feel like reactin' I wanna react the night away
You make me feel like reactin' I wanna react the night away

From Leo Sayer's "You Make Me Feel Like Dancing"

This Electricity

Current, current, current, current flowin' everywhere
Current, current, current, current flowin' everywhere
Flowin' everywhere… flowin' everywhere

I got somethin' called Electricity
Current flows and comes on back to me
And it flows because of Voltage difference
Electrons move from a negative position
Electrons move from a negative position

Current flows… only when the circuits closed
Current flows… only when the circuits closed

Man it don't need you, but you need it
Plug it in let… it go and flow freely
And I don't make um go, I go by *theyself*
And you got some current, and, current flows itself, like nothing else
Yeah, I'm a country boy, but the big city lights fill me up with joy
Ain't life grand playin' with electric toys
Here go that electric song, it's all about those flowin' electrons

Current only flows in only one direction,
From voltage difference after the connection
And I ain't make it, it made me

It's like nuclear force, magnetism, gravity

Current, current, current, current flowin' everywhere
Current, current, current, current flowin' everywhere
Flowin' everywhere, flowin' everywhere.

I got somethin' called Electricity
Current flows and comes on back to me
And it flows because of Voltage difference
Electrons move from a negative position
You know they move from the negative position

Current flows… only when the circuits closed
Current flows… only when the circuits closed

Current flows in unbroken circuits
That's what its called when we close it.
Movin' on electron, blong blong blong
Movin' at the speed of light, whoam whoam whoam
Electrons move easy, flowin' round freely
In a conductor, but not in an insulator
You can't destroy it
You can just change it, through lots-a types of matter
Got these electrons movin' so much faster

Let me shock you in your ear

Charges attract when they're near

Something called induction

Hit the switch, movin' fast

But just in one direction

That's the move that move

That's causin' energy flow

I guaranteed to make lights glow

So do that electric thing baby,

Voltage is da flow chu got,

But you know you're payin'

By the kilowatt (hour)

Makin' that energy,

'Cause you know it make you.

Current, current, current, current flowin' everywhere

Current, current, current, current flowin' everywhere

Flowin' everywhere… flowin' everywhere

I got somethin' called electricity

Current flows and comes on back to me

And it flows because of Voltage difference

Electrons move from a negative position

Electrons move from a negative position

Current flows… only when the circuits closed

Current flows… only when the circuits closed

You know there's two types of circuits,
A series and a parallel
They determine current flow and path it goes
Parallel may have several paths.
But a series just has one,
And Edison had so much fun
I think he found some buried treasured
Yes sir, it's the stuff
Meet me over yonder
Ok, don't play
I'll bring the generator,
You bring your battery
And I'm-a fix it all up,
Movin' all that energy

Current, current, current, current flowin' everywhere
Current, current, current, current flowin' everywhere
Flowin' everywhere… flowin' everywhere

I got somethin' called Electricity
Current flows and comes on back to me
And it flows because of Voltage difference
Electrons move from the negative position
Electrons move from the negative position

Current flows… only when the circuits closed

Current flows… only when the circuits closed

From Bubba Sparks and the Yin Yang Twins' "This New Booty"

Atomic House

Atomic... house
Mighty electrons, spinnin round in a negative cloud
Atomic... house
The nucleus is packed
That's a fact,
Positively holding nothing back.

Atomic... house
One for one, charges balancin',
For every 'lectron there's a proton
They're together everybody knows,
And neutrons fill the empty holes.

You know its got everything
An atom needs to be an element, yeah.
How can it use, the things it use
Protons-neutrons-electrons, what a winning hand!

Element pro-per-ties, the bonding ways,
Make a noble gas wish for electrons to free
It knows it's built to compound if you please
Its the land and the air and all the water in the deep blue sea

Spin around spin around now

Spin around spin around now

Spin around spin around now

Spin around spin around, round, round round

From the Commodores' "Brick House"

A Photon Baby

Well I'm packing up my game and I leaving the sun
Goin' out to the world where there's life and fun
Maybe hit a tree or some phytoplankton
You know its right here where energy comes from
And I'm Mr. Moore, I leave it all on the floor
You'll be a whole lot smarter when leave my door.
I'm westward rollin' across space time
In a tenth of a second I'll go coast to coast
Cain't nothing can catch me, nothing's even close
Come from the sun, I'm a piece of the stars
I'm a photon baby, matter and energy wrapped up in one.
Yea, I'm a photon, baby.
Five hundred ten seconds comin' from the sun
I wanna be a photon baby
I ride across the night sixteen billion miles a day
I wanna be a photon baby
I act like matter but I'm pure energy
Almost all that is, I'm the cause
Wave - particle duality
I'm a photon, baby.

From Kid Rock's "Cowboy"

Metalloid

Finished with my homework
Now my mom will let me out to play
Cause I know 'bout non metals
And metals and what lies between

All along the stair-step line
Semiconductors bid their time
Sometimes they let electrons flow
But other times they hold them tight

I can help you,
Wrinkle up your brain, oh yeah

I don't need much time to show you
Metals all do seem to shine
And they all conduct electrons
And they're malleable and ductile, too

Nobel gases, Halogens
Carbon, O2 and nitrogen
All non metals that I have named
There are more but you are bored

Periodic groups and rows

Tell how elements make their compounds

Seven periods and eighteen groups

All known matter occupies

From Black Sabbath "Paranoid"

Wave

Wave - my scientific obsession
Wave- there's transverse and compression
Wave – it's a rhythmic disturbance,
Wave – with energy as its purpose
Wave – puts the slink in your slinky
wave – count them up with their frequency
Wavelength is one point to another
Watch me wave as they pass through my mother

Wave – when you stop and say hi
Wave – when you turn on the lights
Wave lets me surf at the beach
And I think knowledge is within my reach
They carry light from the stars in the night

Can you see the jiggle in my Jell-O
And the text in my digital lingo
Wave – electromagnetic color
One wave is similar to the other

Wave – when you stop and say hi
Wave – when you turn on the lights
Wave, love of the surf guy
And paints the rainbow in the sky

Ian Lynn Moore, I

Feel the rumbling earthquake
And the heat for your golden brown pancake
Like waves in the pool that you swim in
Wave, radio transmission

Wave – when you stop and say hi
Wave – when you turn on the lights
Wave let me surf at the beach
And bring sound within my reach
They carry light from the stars in the night

From Aerosmith's "Pink"

Mr. Moore

Hey mister mo mister mo mister mo mister
Hey mister mo mister mo mister mo mister

We saw Mr. Moore in the science classroom
Struttin' his stuff on the chalk board.
he said "Hello, you wanna give it a go?"

Yea, so… Get cha googles and ya apron
Get cha googles on right now!
Start collectin' up ya data
Come on do some science with me……..

Voulez-vous apprendre avec moi ce jouer?
Voulez-vous apprendre avec moi?

I stayed in his class while
my brain wrinkled up
I worked through the night…
don't know why
The next thing I knew
I was callin' to you…

Get cha googles and ya apron
Get cha googles on right now!

Ian Lynn Moore, I

Start collectin' up ya data
Come on do some science with me……..

Voulez-vous apprendre avec moi ce jouer?
Voulez-vous apprendre avec moi?

Seeing all those chemicals
Bubbling through
Hazy color neon and blue
Made the scientist that is pent up inside
Roaring until it cried More, More, More
Now I'm doing science at home more
Living a new life of learning
and when he turns off to fall fast asleep
All his memories call: More, More, More

Get cha googles and ya apron
Get cha googles on right now!
Start collectin' up ya data
Come on d some science with me……..
Voulez-vous apprendre avec moi, ce jouer?
Voulez-vous apprendre avec moi?
Voulez-vous apprendre avec moi, ce jouer?
Come on do some science with me.

From Patti Labelle's "Lady Marmalade"

Gravity is Not a Friend

An object moves at a constant speed, forever you see
And one at rest will stay unless acted upon
Its Newton's number 1- Inertia
unless acted upon – Its Newton's number 1- Inertia

The direction of the force tells which way to go
The force equals mass times acceleration
Newton's law number 2 you have found

My momma always told me
Gravity is not your friend
It'll bring you down in the end
You know that it accelerates
At a constant rate
Nine point eight meters per second squared

Forces cause object motion.
There are three laws, inertia is number one,
Then acceleration and action.
Inertia is number one, then acceleration and action.

An action force has an opposite but its just the same
Action/reaction forces all act in pairs
Momentum is velocity times mass

Rockets fly in the air

Because of law number 3 of Newton

Rockets fly in the air, Because of law number 3 of Newton

Newton found all of motion laws

And there are three

They govern how things move around

Even you and me

Forces cause all motion Isaac Newton found

My momma always told me

Gravity is not your friend

It'll bring you down in the end

You know that it accelerates

At a constant rate

Nine point eight meters

Per second squared

Forces cause object motion.

There are three laws, inertia is number one,

Then acceleration and reaction.

From Michael Jackson "Billie Jean"

Transverse Waves

Back row learner,
Always hidin' in the corner,
And I never would raise my hand.
A class clown loser,
Never made above an 80,
But I never much cared about grades
When somebody told me,
"There's a whole light spectrum,
Most of which we can't even see,"
Now the best times I'm havin'
With reflection and refraction
And it started with ROY G BIV
Light this!

Rainbow streatchin'
all across the sky
Little prisms up in the air
Singin' "twinkle, twinkle"
Now my brains got a wrinkle
And I can't believe I didn't care
So, I took a big chance in my science class
And my momma, she was so amazed
My teacher won't foolin'
'Cause she knew what she was doin'

And she told me bout transverse waves

When he told me 'bout…

Radio waves,

Gamma rays,

Microwaves waves,

Those X rays,

Infrared,

Ultra-violet,

Electromag—netic waves

And that's ROY G BIV

Light this!

A transverse wave

Has got a crest and a trough

At a right angle to the wavelength

Crest at the top, trough at the bottom

You measure amplitude from the rest

When you turn up the frequency

You increase the power

Turn it down

To stretch the wavelength

And my next door neighbor

You know I saw he had a laser

And it started with ROY G BIV

Light this!

Three hundred thousand

Kilometer per second

Electromagnetism sets that pace

Racing from the sun

In under nine seconds

It can go through matter and space

You know we know a whole lot

But we've just begun

To understand the sun's fusion

Like dark things absorb

But white does reflecting

The colors you can separate

Radio waves,

Gamma rays,

Microwaves waves,

Those X rays,

Infrared,

Ultra-violet,

Electromag—netic waves

And that's ROY G BIV

Light this!

From Aerosmith's "Walk This Way"

Sail Your Boat

Well, I'd like to know about sailboat motion
I said, I'd like to know about sailboat motion

Sail the boat,
What moves the boat baby?
Sail the boat,
Don't tip the boat over?
Sail the boat,
What moves the boat baby?
Sail the boat-t-t-t-t

Wind is what a sail boat needs for speed.
Water friction might cause low velocity,
But you can make the more hydrodynamicly.
Sail size and shape can make it fly like a jet ski.

Energy causes ship motion,
Wind resistance and some friction; action reaction.

Now, I think I know about sailboat motion.
I said, I think I know about sailboat motion.

Sail the boat,
What moves the boat baby?

Sail the boat,
Don't tip the boat over?
Sail the boat,
What moves the boat baby?
Sail the boat-t-t-t-t

Momentum equals mass times velocity
And when two object collide they conserve energy
For every motion there is an equal and opposite
Energy's never destroyed, we just transfer it.

Sail the boat,
What moves the boat baby?
Sail the boat,
Don't tip the boat over?
Sail the boat,
What moves the boat baby?
Sail the boat-t-t-t-t

From The Hues Corporation's "Rock the Boat"

Welcome to the Lab Room

Welcome to the lab room
Where were learnin' every day
'Bout the universe mechanical
And all the chemicals by name
This is the place you'll need to be
For chances and mistakes
If you'll all get dirty and wet
you'll see your mind free.

In the lab room,
Welcome to the lab room.
Watch it wrinkle up your…
Ba, ba, ba, ba, ba, ba, ba, brain,…brain!
I wanna see you learn.

Guns n Roses "Welcome to the Jungle"

Cellular

There bigger than molecules,

they're the smallest organization of living things

They're what make you

and all plants and birds and monarons

They're in your spleen

and even in the smallest lima bean

I think you've figured out

That I'm talkin' bout cells

They've organelles

This is cellular, cellular night

There ain't no second chances

Once it makes it on the slide, yea

Cellular, cellular night

We'll even add some dye in

So you can see them

In the

Light.

If you've a cell wall,

Large vacuoles

And chloroplast

Than you're plant cell,

Makin' food and oxygen for you.

They're everywhere,
They're in tallest trees
And they're plankton
And it's the sun
Where they get their energy
And they're all green

This is cellular, cellular night
There ain't no second chances
Once it make it on the slide, yea
Cellular, cellular night
We'll even add some dye in
So you can see them
In the
Light.

All cells are basically the same, they've many similar parts
Cell membranes and nuclei, Golgi bodies and vacuoles
DNA and chromosomes they fill the world both night and day
They're everywhere in sight

If you can't make food,
Mitochondria will process it for you
If you've no cell wall
That's because you're an animal
Now is the time

For you to understand the major difference

Between you and the plants eat for energy,

You're not green

This is cellular, cellular night

There ain't no second chances

Once it make it on the slide, yea

Cellular, cellular night

We'll even add some dye in

So you can see them

In the

Light.

From Michael Jackson's "Thriller"

Red Hot

Sizzlin', red hot Mista Moore, yea
Ready for me, ready or not... want what I got.
All da world, all da girls, all da boys...
All da students, Mista Moore say...

Temperature measures particle motion
The hotter it is the more that they're movin'
Heat is the energy that's keepin' you warm
Conduction, (con)vection and radiation.

It comes from da sun... Radiation and causes jubilation.
It moves in transverse waves,
Through matter and space down on every nation
You can't hold them down,
But you can use them now for da microwave oven
And in Jamaica man it's hot like the Sun.

Heat is the one that moves through convection,
Me tell you brotha...
It moves from hot to cold,
If I can be so bold there can be no other....
Because its flowin' round up and down,
And movin' through your motha..
No lie temp sets da speed for movin' energy.

Man don't say me crazy now,
Direct contact's how conduction moves the heat..
Like in da summer time when you move your feet
To keep um off da street...
Child there's no playin' know,
Molecules move 'round when they meet
When it's touchin' its the way to go...
To make da energy flow.....

When you roll with a teacher like me...
with a brotha like me, there's no other
No matta how small da mass
the thermal energy lasts it goes undercover
For me it's a blast that your learnin' now
And you wanna discover..
Everything out about heat
Now you wanna hear when me utter...

Temperature measures particle motion
The hotter it is the more that they're movin'
Heat is the energy that's keepin' you warm
Conduction, (con)vection and radiation.

From Sean Paul's "Temperature"

You Matter

Matter, Matter
Solid, liquid, plasma, gas
Anything with space and mass
Look at me, I'm matter
I matter
Matter

Fourteen billion years have passed
But still this stuff it lasts and lasts
Its splashed across the universe
All that ever was is here
People think reuse is new
But its just what the cosmos do

Conservation… of matter

Love to learn, intelligence
And science, math and NoS,
And lots and lots of technology
Look at you, you matter
Matter matters
Matter

All this chitter-chatter,

'Bout space and matter,

Chitter-chatter 'bout

Space and matter,

And technology

We're givin' it away out here on 12th street

Because it matters

Work and work

For hopes and dreams

Ain't you hungry for

Success, success, success, success

Its matter! (matter) and it matters!

You matter. You matter

Ahhh, look at you, you matter

Its about matter

Look at me- its about matter, yeah

Protons, neutrons, electrons

Listen up and sing along

Atoms, quarks and molecules

Still obey periodic rules

But only 92

Kinds of matter, yeah

We find in nature,

That's all the matter

That's all the matter, uh-huh

This stuff matters, uh-huh,

You matter

From The Rolling Stones "Shattered"

Elements

Elements
I got elements, I got elements.

One hundred and twelve known elements,
Giving matter its mass and a substance
It's a solid, a liquid, a gas,
All their atoms are makin' up the mass

One atom is connected to another atom.
When atoms combine they form a molecule
When atoms combine, it's an elemental rule.
Before you know it they're makin' ions, too.

One hydrogen connected to one hydrogen
Two hydrogens connected to one oxygen
H_2O molecules for me and you
One oxygen connected to one oxygen
Two oxygens connected to one carbon
CO_2 molecules is what you get
That's carbon dioxide, that I breath for you

Sodium connected to the chlorine
NaCl we use to make ice cream
That's sodium chloride, table salt

Ian Lynn Moore, I

Eating NaCl to make my food taste good
One hundred and twelve known elements
Giving matter its mass and substance
It's a solid, a liquid, a gas,
Their atoms combine makin' up the mass

From Sonny and Cher's "I Got You, Babe"

Gravity

You know that gravity
Is gonna keep your feet
Safe on the ground
Cause that's what Newton found

When an apple's in the air
It will fall without a care, yeah
But if in space it's hangin' round
It may never hit the ground, oh yeah
Forces act both near and far
In the sky and in your car, yeah

Gravity's got lots to do
It holds on me and the moon, yeah
Ocean tides as they flow,
The planets spinnin' as they go, yeah

There's lots of gravity from the sun, yeah
And you know there's a formula
Masses by distance between squared
Times nine point eight meters per second squared

Weight is caused by gravity
To pull on mass is what it needs, yea

It acts on giants and grains of sand
And even causes projectile motion"

Gravity will keep your feet
Safe on the ground where they should be

From Earth Wind and Fire's "Shining Star"

Sputnikolor Dreams

THE TRUTH ACORDING TO MR. S'MORE

Sputnikolor Dreams

SOL

Words slam against my eyes
Like arrows on a city wall besieged.
Trebuchet lofted ideas
Assail my consciousness

At first they came in peace,
Bound on thick chew proof cardboard
Big and bold, simple and concise,
Apples for "A", Spot running with Dick and Jane.

We traded and engaged in commerce,
Mine for theirs, theirs for mine.
We partnered, married even.
So in love, the cosmos was at our feet.

Then something changed.
Learning wasn't enough.
There was data to analyze,
Criteria and objectives to master

A,B,C's became a, b, c or d,
Learning became standardized,
Standards became tests,
And tests replaced learning.

Now I stare at the glowing slate

Trying to see the face I once adored

Hidden amongst the curses and cursors

Or on one of the four roads I've been given to travel.

I don't want to be left behind.

I want to win the race to the top.

I've taken my SOLs so I should be happy, right?

But mostly I just feel "Shit Out of Luck."

Fourteen

I was fourteen, once

Hanging around outside the 7-11

Waiting for someone we knew

To buy us something

We couldn't on our own

Smokin' and jokin'

And dreaming

Tomorrow was all there was

But today wouldn't die

I was fourteen, once

I was fourteen, once

When all that mattered

Was that pretty face

In History class

 Or maybe it was Geometry

School was just a place to hide

Behind the desks,

Between the classes

No one much noticed me

Through silent whispers I'd scream

I was fourteen, once

I was fourteen, once.

Though most of it I've long forgot.

The trips to the mall

 For God knows what,

All day calls about nothing at all.

Who was I then,

Did I want to be me?

I think there should be a medal

For those who survive 14

Like me… and you. Hopefully.

I was fourteen, once.

Rapturous Morning

Peering out the window into the still dark morning.

Tracing the familiar lines for any sign, any at all

There in the silent blackness, a white blanket.

Down the stairs like the vandal hoards,

The flick of the switch, a momentary static hum,

The pictures comes into focus

A blue strip courses across the bottom of the screen.

"Closed" it says!

Hands in the air, running throughout the house.

Screaming a triumphant battle cry

Like Sitting Bull after the Little Bighorn

To the basement for our chariots:

Radio Flyer, snow disc, old card board boxes

Skis from the Goodwill.

My wife shakes her head and puts on coffee and cocoa,

peering out the window

At the rapturous morning.

The Truth about Water

You have heard it said: "Thousands have lived without love, but not one has lived without water." (W.H. Auden)
But I tell you the truth, "life without love isn't worth living."

You have heard it said: "Water, water everywhere, but not a drop to drink" (Samuel Taylor Coleridge)
But I tell you the truth, "Its not the water that kills you but what's in it."

You have heard it said: "You can lead a horse to water, but you can't make him drink" (12 Century English proverb)
But I tell you the truth, "Sometimes you should listen to your horse."

You have heard it said: "Rain makes corn, corn makes whiskey, and whiskey"… well helps with procreation. (Luke Bryan)
But I tell you the truth, "Be careful with whom you stand in the rain."

You have heard it said: "Still waters run deep."
(Idom L cica 1200 CE)
But I tell you the truth, "Still waters breed mosquitoes."

You have heard it said: "Wait thirty minutes before you go swimming" (Your momma)

But I tell you the truth, "Wait a little longer if you don't know how to swim."

You have heard it said: "Before enlightenment, chop wood, carry water. After enlightenment, chop wood, carry water." (Zen saying)
But I tell you the truth, "True enlightenment is a heat pump and indoor plumbing"

You have heard it said: "Fire, water and government know nothing of mercy." (Albanian proverb)
But I tell you the truth, "Don't forget mother-in-laws and ex-wives"

You have heard it said: "There is no life without water."
But I tell you the truth, "There is no life without love, water just keeps it lubricated."

You have heard it said: "Water is the only drink for a wise man." (Henry David Thoreau)
But I tell you the truth, "Wisdom is overrated."

Deer

Deer
Predator prey
Good for dinner
Not for my hood
Deer

Punnett Squares

I have a friend who has four daughters

All four are beautiful and bright

Obviously from the same potter

They've their mother's eyes and witty bite

Of course they have her chromosomes

This pair of Xs is not her size

Though after four she'd not be alone

But there's something else that this implies

Then I saw this thing from Mendel's view

These traits plugged into squares

One little fact I'd not thought through

All Xs equal all X pairs

So, from the data, I've surmised,

My friend's a girl, to his wife's surprise.

Meal Ticket

Under the porch light
Electromagnetic glow
Toad waits for dinner'

Green Hawaiian

In my second year of teaching, actually my first full year, I saw on my rolls a name I recognized, "Jacob McDonald." The son of my primary science education professor from college, whom I greatly respected and in spite of his slight build always intimidating to me because seemed to know all my tricks and trump me whenever I tried to stray from the path he'd laid out. On registration night I was petrified, he and his wife came in my classroom. She asked a few questions that I was thankfully able to answer, picked up a supplies list and turn to her husband, my mentor and just said, "Honey?" I knew what she meant was, "Do you have anything to add or questions you want to ask?" but her scarcity of words was met in kind.

> He glanced around fast
> As I waited for his words
> "I think you need plants"

That was it, I turned my head and craned my good ear towards him so I'd have a better chance to catch whatever wisdom I knew this giant upon whom he stood would utter, but there was nothing but the except the dust settling back on the floor from where he whisked off down the hall. What did it mean? Was it, "Great job, you just need to green it up in here a little." Or did he mean, "You're kidding me, this is the best you can do after all that time in my class. At least get a plant, for Pete sake."

> So, off to Wal-Mart I did fly
> For some chlorophyll to buy
> All through the store I scoured
> Not for silk flowers
> Or paper fronds plastic leaves
> Only a plant would make me leave
> There in the back door corner stood
> A plant display of solid wood

I bought four: an aloe plant a jade plant, some grass looking stuff, and another thing with "Hawaiian" in its name. There was a reason I didn't have plants in my room, why I don't garden, in fact, only black mold grows on bread at my house. Needless to say the grass turned to amber waves within two weeks, the jade plant went to sleep with its ancestors not too long after that and the aloe didn't stand a chance to make it though the Bunsen burner labs after Christmas. By June, the only one that remained was the Hawaiian thing with the leaves that vaguely resembled something on a Bob Marley t-shirt, but it was quickly losing those. I took the pathetic thing home and my wife began her nurse routine.

> "All you need is a little water."
> She spoke to the plant in hushed tones.
> "Here, drink it in, have some sun."

And I'll be darned, it grew
Summer turned to fall
Time to take it…
Back to school
I thought.
No?

Gingerly, I packed it into the box of books I was taking back to school and tried to sneak out the door until I heard, "Umm Honey, where is my plant?" "It's my school plant." I answered. "WAS' your school plant until you tried to kill it." At that point I knew I had abdicated even though I continued my protest for a few more symbols.

More than a decade has passed since I relinquished custody of that little piece of Hawaii and it is still conducting photo synthesis, still making oxygen still occupying its stately perch by the kitchen window. I never tried to replace it and if my old college mentor ever comes back to visit I hope he has something more to say than, "I think you need a plant."

Rusty Wire

A rusty barbed wire

Separating wild from not

On cedar posts strung

The Epistle to Kay, Who's No Longer Here

Dear Kay,

    I visited the church where they read your eulogy. My wife's college choir had their reunion there. I sat near the same seat I had that day. It seems like a life time ago but just yesterday. They sounded like angels, I hope you enjoyed it. The last time I was here you were clothed in cherry and off white taffeta with a train of flowers surrounding you. The pews were filled with children and the air wet with sorrow. It still haunts me.

    It was just a few days before that we were on the sideline together screaming at those other girls, "shoot," "pass the ball," "get it out of there." You know the stuff coaches yell. Remember? I didn't let you play, you had gotten into trouble in some other teacher's class and I was being a good coach and teaching you that academics come first. I guess you never had time to use what you learned. You soldiered through and cheered on your friends as we were handed our hats. Did we win a game that whole year? Would you still be here if you had played that day?

    Then this might be your wedding day and I somehow vetted in. Maybe not to the reception, I'd not rank that high, but for a toaster or a Ralph Lauren towel you'd send me a card. Those same children who cried their rivers that day would be here today instead to cheer and drink and yes some would cry, but that would be OK.

    I want to ask you, if I can, what were you thinking that day? I guess maybe you really weren't. Were you angry? Were you sad? Was there nothing worth the effort it took to wake up? I guess not.

I came to see you while you were sleeping, your mom and dad were there with preachers and doctors. I only glimpsed your face through the wires, lights and hoses and I only stayed a moment. I couldn't bear it and you never knew.

I so desperately want to hear someone call out across Wal-Mart, "Mr. Moore." For them to come closer and say, "Do you remember me?" For me to pretend I do as I search behind the adult façade for the little girl I knew for 47 minutes a day that year so long ago. I want to say, "I remember your face," when it is only barely true and ask for your name. "Of course I remember you," I would reply, but you would have really faded into the furrows in my face and the grey in my beard.

I want to forget the flowers, the speeches and the prayers. I want to forget you like I was supposed to, like, in time, I will all the rest. But I never can, because here you are, still etched in my mind, clothed in cherry and off white taffeta.

Forever Yours,

If Only

If only I were taller or smarter
If only I were young and light
If only I'd been good
If only I'd tried
If only...

If only I'd have stepped up and spoke up
If only I'd opened my eyes
If only I would go
If only I'd stay
If only...

If only I'd have sat down and shut up
If only I'd taken a breath
If only, if only
I would still ask
If only...

Voiceless

She slipped in with her pointed escort and handed me a slip of paper
I tried to read the name printed there but the syllables didn't seem to make sense to my tongue.
I asked her her name but my mind refused to remember
I motion to an empty seat, to the back corner she was flung.

Forty seven minutes she'd sit there everyday
Trying to soak in what I would offer without hear ears to guide
Indeed, She could hear and laugh she had so much to say
But no one would listen, no one cared, no one would take her side.

I glanced her way from time to time
And often would surmise
The barriers 'tween her and me were much to high to climb
so she faded from my mind then unnoticed from my eyes

Voiceless, Voiceless; I gave no heed.
Voiceless, Voiceless, my soul should bleed.

The Epistle to Ray, in Prison

Dear Ray,

    I saw your picture on the TV today, there in living room in living color, with that scowl you get on your face when you are angry, scared, or confused. I guess I saw that look a lot when you were here, but you are a long way from middle school now. You would be talking to some other boy about football or going to the NBA and I would call you on it and you would get that look. You would blurt out an answer you thought for sure was right, but I would shake my head and I'd see that face. I saw that same pose when you were waiting in the office after getting in a fight over someone talking about your mom. Yeah, that was the look I saw, just a little angrier, a little more scared and a little more confused.

    That look wasn't the only one I remember. That big toothy smile you would stretch across you face when you got a good grade, I want to see that one again; or maybe the sparkle reflecting in your eyes from the striker when you lit your Bunsen burner for the first time. Even that shy grin when you passed a note under you desk to that girl you liked so much. What was her name, I can picture her but I can't recall her name.

    So, what happened? I guess they said what you did and I want to protest and say you couldn't have, but I'd be lying. But not everyone who fits the stereo type turn out that way. You could have done things differently, couldn't you? What was going through your head when you pulled the trigger? My God, what were you thinking after? I can't get over how you looked on T.V. You looked so much like that kid I met when you where, what, 12 or 13, when you walked into class with that same angry, scared, confused look on your face; just a little angrier, a little more scared and a little more confused.

So, what now, sentencing, appeal, concrete, steel bars and barbed wire? I thought I heard something about a capital offense. I shuddered. I wanted so much more for you. You wanted so much more for you. There was so much more you could have been or done or even just tried. Was there something I could have done different to help you steer a different course or was you fate sealed before you got to me, before I saw that look on your face, the same one I saw on T.V.

I hope they are treating you well, the bed is comfortable and the food is OK. I've never heard anyone complain about prison food. At least not like they talk about school cafeterias, airline "meals" and Army mess hall, but maybe there are other issues more pressing than Salisbury steak when you are there. I don't think I want to imagine what it is like. What are they telling you? I mean the judge and your lawyer. I don't know much about your case. Only what they said on the news and what I saw in your angry, scared, confused face.

Write me back if you get a chance. Let me know if I can do something for you, your mom or your brother. How are they, anyway? She always had such high hopes for you. He always looked up to you. What did you tell them? "I'm sorry?" What does that mean after this?

"I'm sorry," is all I can say, Ray. I'm sorry I didn't reach you when I knew you were struggling. I'm sorry didn't find you when I knew you were lost. I'm sorry I didn't pick you up when I knew you'd fallen. I'm sorry I wasn't there to take the gun from your hands or to chase the thoughts from your head that forced you there. I'm sorry I can't unbuckle the belts from your arms and legs or take the needle from your vein. I'm sorry that all too soon your face will fade from my memory as someone new takes your place with that same angry, scared confused look on their face as they walk into my classroom or on T.V.

Forever Your Friend

The Congregation of the Mighty

I stood in the congregation of the mighty with the children of God.
Sitting in judgment over creation,
Our arrogance eclipsed even the sun.
As I looked down from our tertiary throne,
Our empire, built on the backs of giants, won by the sweat of their fathers,
And nurtured on the breast of their mothers, covered the cosmos;
But we've looted the coffers and banquet on, now, but bare bones.
Our minds have titrated until they glow hot pink,
Neutralized by years of trivia, impotent with mediocrity,
Not hot nor cold, but spewed out luke-warm boredom.
"Awake, awake from your gluttonous slumber,"
I call to myself, we who once mastered the universe.
"Awake, awake from your death rattle lethargy,"
 I whisper to me, we whom God made in His image.
But I cannot answer, I am chained to my stupor,
The violent determination housed in my DNA
Is rotted by this generation of morbid torpidity.
The stench has called to the fungi and worms
Who consume me while I still breathe
And to the dust I return.
My funeral fire is lit while my blood still courses
And into ash I fall.
But from death comes life,

From the grave comes sustenance,

And as the sun sets so does it rise.

In the end, there is no end

All matter and energy is conserved,

Hope is always salvaged,

Faith arises from the embers,

And out of affliction is found the path to the promise land.

Judged by creation and compelled to repentance

Under the radiance of the sun,

I stood in the congregation of the mighty with the children of God.

Hornets

Hornets

Yellow black

Grey paper bell

Carbon-dioxide seeking missiles

Hornets

Cosmos Cake

I want my cake and eat it, too.
I need to believe and to know
I want to look at the Cosmos
And see God sow the universe

Will it rip space and time to say,
"I want my cake and eat it, too."
Did not God say "Let there be Light,"
And Steven, "There was a Big Bang."

We exchange bow shots and rim shots,
Pulpit to chalk board and back, but…
I want my cake and eat it, too.
For there's reason in the chaos.

From belfries and ivory towers
Chrome fish fight their circular war,
But all creation testifies
"I want my cake and eat it, too"

Friendly Fire

The battle rages everywhere
For mind and body, every hair
Fight the beast called ignorance
For our kids minds we wage defense
Seed, sewer, and I make three
Educational holy trinity
This force we've formed from common care
But friendly fire killed me there.

Option 7 and CBA's

Zoe's got a new tattoo
I think that it's her mother's name
Yasmine's phone's been disconnected
For the third time this year
Xavier hides out in the back
I'm not sure I've heard him speak

William thinks we all hate him
'Cause I won't let him fail
Vic left in a cop squad car
Said it was a bb gun
Ulanda quietly withdrew
I heard she had a boy

Tyrone thinks he's NBA bound
He's only four feet three
Shaniqua's brother is in the pen
She acts like she don't care
Ronald tries to sleep through class
But we force him go home

Quentin's always drawing guns
He always looks so sad
Pierson never has a book

He's checked out instead
In Nigel's blood there is more lead
Than in regular gasoline

Mary is out of paper
She can't afford some more
Leah's stuck on all the boys
It just depends on who's in sight
A drive-by shot up Jacob's house
No one said if he's alright

Ian's mom has moved again
I'm not sure he knows where
Hannah always comes late
She has to go court today
Gini wishes for her dad
But she's better off this way

Frankie's never made an A
I'm not sure what he'd do
Elijah really's got no clue
But tries and tries and tries
Donte shows up once a week
You know his grandma passed away

Casey was put into a home
She says she hates her folks
Beth always hides her wrists
And whispers to herself
Adam's got too many bruises
And tries to be too cool

The DOE says it's all my fault
I guess I'll take the blame
So, I can come another day
And give shelter from the rain

Wire

Wire
Rusty barbed
Cedar post strung
'tween wild and not
Wire

Birthday Cake

Who doesn't like cake, in some form: ice cream cake, chocolate cake, carrot cake, cheese cake, or just any flavor birthday cake? I sure do and my favorite is orange cake with orange icing. Weird, I know but that's what I've gotten for my birthday every day since I was four. No one has told me for sure, but I've seen pictures of a Florida vacation around that time and maybe, just maybe, those big tangy-sweet, tree fresh orbs, fresh from my great grand-fathers front yard tree stuck with me and; go figure, I wanted an orange cake. Honestly, good old Duncan Hines is good enough for me. Now, "old" in this sentence is like "old faithful" but not exclusive of the "My God, how long has this been on the shelf at the neighborhood grocery store?" usage. Admittedly, there was always a hint of baby aspirin aftertaste, but most of the time that translated into more for me.

I got married and things changed. I still get my cake but it doesn't look or really even taste like the "Bayer" version I grew up with. My wife is from south Philadelphia and along with her slightly odd accent she brought an expectation that food actually taste good. The diverse culinary culture that she grew up with had evolved her pallet beyond what most homo sapiens could ever expect. I am not at all trying to belittle my mom, but my parents taught at a boarding school where it was an expectation of the faculty that they eat most meals in the dining hall and thank heaven because we would have starved or died of charcoaled food poisoning. So, the first time my amped up cake was laid out in front of me it was almost afraid to eat it. That multi layered, zest infused, cream cheese and mandarin orange slathered, master piece of a *flavogasm* is all I could have ever dream of. Needless to say, I am left significantly less cake for the after party snack than I was growing up, but it is my cake and I get to eat it, at least some of it.

Here in lies a problem, I expect to "have my cake and eat it, too;" and I'm not afraid to apply this principle in to other areas of my life. I am a Christian, not just by geographic, cultural and genetic placement, but by choice and I endeavor to allow what that means to me to evolve accordingly. One of the things that I have become convinced of is that God gave me a scientific mind and to look out at the cosmos from any other vantage point would deny the gifts he has given me.

I accept, without reservation, that God made the universe and everything in it. I believe that "creation" happened just the way it is described in Genesis. However, I don't think that anyone has a clue how to interpret, scientifically or even chronologically, what was written in scripture for the ears and minds of a Bronze Age audience. So, I am equally persuaded that a scenario, closely resembling the current "Big Bang" theory and its time frame is the best scientific explanation. I can't be the only one who sees that the scientific definition of the Big Bang theory supports the Judeo-Christian belief that everything that ever was, is, and ever will be was flung into "being" at one instant. Call it what you will but that sounds like an awfully big bang.

Up until recently science has held the high ground ever since the Scopes Trial debacle where even though the powers that be staved off the teaching of Evolution in public schools for a few more years, it was obvious to most onlookers that the whole thing was a witch hunt. And just like the dogma of seventeenth century Salem, the fever pitched attach against these novel ideas has waned until now most people accept, to varying degrees, Darwin's ideas.

The problem now is that many in the scientific community have dipped into the inquisitioner's bag of tricks and looks inward at its data and outward at its detractors with the same blind religious fervor that would have made Galileo shudder at the full circle we have made.

This battle of arrogance and ignorance at its rawest form is played out on bumper stickers and little those chrome decals, stick fish versus stick fish with legs. It's Dr. Seuss all over again, remember The *Sneaches* with "stars on thars." Maybe one of the most important Scientific/Theological debates where we try to address true questions of faith and reason being fought at the same level as "My Kid Can Kick Your Honor Student's Ass" and everybody is slinging mud. How this level of contempt beneficial to anyone? How does "My Fish Can Eat Your Fish," show Christian love and charity?

Conversely, how does it show some evolved our primal state into a higher being?

How about a new take on some ancient wisdom? "Love your neighbor, no matter who his uncle and come to my birthday party and have a piece of cake. I'll even let you eat it, too.

Cellular Secrets

Darkness fall across the lab
The bussing hour is close at hand
But who so ever though they would
Stay back for some extra good
The microscopes are all turned off
And Mr. Moore's off playing golf
They're still lurking everywhere
With flagella and cilia hair
Confined in membranes and cell walls
With single cells and volvox balls
And though they fight to stay alive
All through the waters that they strive
Just to live another day
To flow around the creek and play
Floating in the dark pond waters'
They never make a sound
...The secrets of the cellular.

Fire with Fire

Sometimes I don't know what's wrong with these kids

It's like their mommas BET and they don't know who they daddy is

I don't know why, but they just don't get it

I try to teach um something' but they always forget it

It ain't like I'm trying give 'em something they never gonna use

'Cause most of what I am I owe to a teacher in school

And the only thing the streets gave me was heart ache and road rash

And every now and then I'm still picking glass

Outta my forehead from when I hit that tree

You know I should a died that night but Jesus carried me

And now I standing up here with a book in one hand

And a little scrap of chalk, fightin'.

Fire with fire, hoping that you'll climb a little higher

Fightin' fire with fire. Trying to make your future a little brighter

Its not like I'm trying be all hip hop, flip flop

Acting like I'm smoking rock

I'm just trying to get through

Show um what they need to do

Cause this world keeps spinning round and round

And you gotta start running when your feet hit the ground

That time is coming baby, ready or not

I just don't want your crib to be a cell block

Ian Lynn Moore, I

Don't wanna see your name on channel two
With a list of all the things you thought you had to do
Just to keep the bill collectors from calling
Asking why you don't try to fight.

Fire with fire, hoping that you'll climb a little higher
Fightin' fire with fire, Trying to make your life a little brighter

You don't make your friends, they make you
You can lie to yourself, but I'll tell you the truth
Do you think your momma really wants to see you
Living on Clay St. surrounded by concrete
And barbed wire somebody watching every thing you do
Now I know I'm talking worst case scenario
But, If I see you in the mall all bloated out pregnant
Ready to pop any day, I feel like I have failed you
And wonder if there was something I could have done or
Said to beat some sense into that thick head
You got all decorated up in beads and shells, braids and dreads
But you never turned on, you never hit the switch
But I keep on…fightin' fire.

ABOUT THE AUTHOR

Ian Moore is a father of five, happily married, middle school science teacher in Lynchburg, VA. He has been teaching 7th Grade Physical Science since 2000 at Paul Laurence Dunbar Middle School for Innovation. He and to his wife Debbie life near the Blue Ridge Parkway in Amherst County with their youngest son Jackson, two dogs, a cat and an occasional cow who wonders across the yard. At Dunbar he is the faculty sponsor for WDMS, the schools Television studio, coaches football and occasionally soccer.

Ian is a Veteran of the U.S. Army where he served as a tank mechanic at Ft Carson, Colorado in the late 80's. Upon exiting the service in 1988 worked various construction, service and manufacturing jobs while plodding through college, one or two classes at a time, and taking several semesters off at random points. In 1997, when the sheet metal fabrication factory he was working in closed without notice, he seized upon the opportunity to finish his undergraduate degree in Middle School Education from Lynchburg College.

In 2000, he published his first poem, "Coffee Stains," in the Prism, L.C.'s literary magazine. The poem was reprinted in 2012, in magazine's Anniversary Edition highlighting 85 years of the school's literary tradition and with only a handful of the college's authors. During the twelve years between the first and second printing of "Coffee Stains" his writing was primarily focused on meeting the curriculum needs of his students at Dunbar. He wrote dozens of songs and poems about learning science and science content in hopes that the information would more readily sink in. However, after he receiving a copy of the reprint, he realized that his work may have a broader appeal and that he may have more to communicate than just the structure of an atom.

He began to write feverishly and Sputnikolor Dreams was realized The sixty-six piece, three chapter collection has drawn together many of the songs and poems that I had written for his students. It also tells their stories and offers readers a window into the author's classroom and even wrestles with his own internal debates between religion and science. The title and release date coincided with the fifty-fifth anniversary of the Soviet Sputnik Satellite launch that has had such a profound impact on science and education in the United States.

Made in the USA
Charleston, SC
31 October 2012